Lightning
BOLT
BOOKS™

Let's Look at Iguanas

Judith Jango-Cohen

Lerner Publications Company
Minneapolis

Lerner Publications Company
A division of Lerner Publishing Group, Inc.
241 First Avenue North
Minneapolis, MN 55401 U.S.A.

Website address: www.lernerbooks.com

Library of Congress Cataloging-in-Publication Data

Jango-Cohen, Judith.
    Let's look at iguanas / by Judith Jango-Cohen.
      p. cm. — (Lightning bolt books™—Animal close-ups)
    Includes index.
    ISBN 978-0-7613-3888-8 (lib. bdg. : alk. paper)
    1. Desert iguana—Juvenile literature. I. Title.
  QL666.L25J36 2010
  597.95'421754—dc22   2008051857

Manufactured in the United States of America
1 2 3 4 5 6 — BP — 15 14 13 12 11 10

Contents

A Scaly Reptile

Look at those claws and that bumpy skin! Is this a dinosaur?

No! This animal is an iguana. Iguanas are reptiles.

Some reptiles have short, stubby legs—like this iguana. Other reptiles, like snakes, have no legs at all.

Reptiles have scaly skin.
Scales are hard like your nails.
They help hold in water.

Hard scales protect iguanas
and other reptiles.

With scaly skin, reptiles can live in dry places. They can live in hot places too. **Where do iguanas live?**

Hot places make good homes for some iguanas.

These iguanas live near the sea. Other iguanas live in rain forests.

Desert iguanas live in the hot and dry desert.

Desert iguanas live in the deserts of the southwestern United States and northern Mexico.

Basking Iguanas

Most desert animals rest in the shade in the hot afternoon. What do desert iguanas do?

Desert iguanas bask in the sun in the hot afternoon.

Iguanas bask to stay warm. **Iguanas are ectotherms.** Ectotherms cannot make their own body heat. Their body heat changes to match the warmth or cold around them.

This iguana lies on a warm rock in the sun.

An iguana cools off in the shade.

Climbing Iguanas

Even a desert iguana can get too hot. Then it climbs into a shady bush to cool off.

The iguana uses its claws to climb. The claws of an iguana are sharp. They grip the bark.

An iguana's sharp claws allow it to easily hold onto branches.

An iguana finds food in the bushes.

Desert iguanas eat leaves, fruits, and flowers.

This iguana has a mouthful of cactus!

Iguana Territories

An iguana eats and basks in its territory.

A territory is an iguana's very own place. An iguana keeps other iguanas out of its territory.

An iguana keeps a sharp eye out for other animals in its territory.

A desert iguana can be hard to see in its territory. The iguana's skin blends in with the stones, sand, and trees.

Animals that blend in
with their background are
camouflaged.

Can you find the
camouflaged iguana
hiding here?

Iguana Predators

A camouflaged iguana can hide from predators. Predators are animals that hunt and eat other animals.

Roadrunners hunt and eat iguanas.

An iguana can fight
predators with its claws.

It can also flick its
tail like a whip.

An iguana may run if it does not want to fight. But what if a predator grabs the iguana by the tail?

These iguanas are on the watch for predators.

Snap! Its tail drops off, and the iguana keeps running. Soon a new tail may grow back.

Iguanas sometimes grow a new tail after their original tail breaks off.

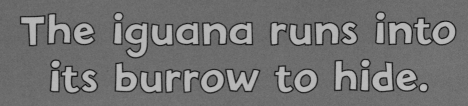

The iguana runs into
its burrow to hide.
A burrow is a hole that the
iguana digs in the sand.

Baby Iguanas

Desert iguanas lay their eggs in burrows. Then one day, the eggs hatch. What do baby iguanas look like?

These iguana eggs are safe inside a burrow.

Baby iguanas have long tails, scales, and sharp claws. They look like little dinosaurs!

Desert Iguana Range Map

Desert iguana range

Desert Iguana Diagram

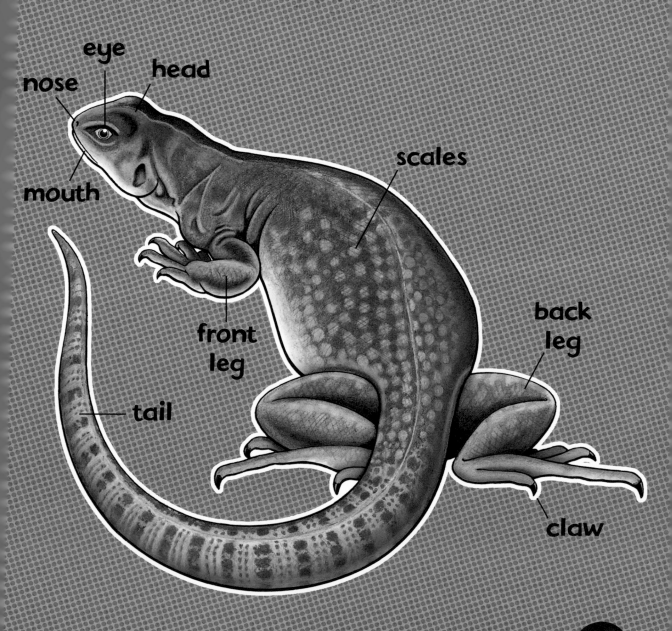

nose

eye

head

mouth

scales

front leg

tail

back leg

claw

Glossary

bask: to lie in the sun to warm the body. Iguanas must bask to stay alive.

burrow: a hole that an iguana digs in the ground. Iguanas hide and lay their eggs in burrows.

camouflage: coloring or covering that helps an animal blend in with its surroundings

desert: a dry, sandy region that gets little rain

ectotherm: an animal whose body heat changes to match the warmth or cold around it

predator: an animal that hunts and eats other animals

reptile: a crawling or creeping animal that has a backbone. Most reptiles have scaly skins and lay eggs.

scale: a flat, hard plate on an iguana's skin. Scales protect a reptile's body and hold in water.

territory: an animal's very own place. An iguana keeps other iguanas out of its territory.

Further Reading

Aronsky, Jim. *All about Lizards.* New York: Scholastic, 2004.

Buckingham, Suzanne. *Meet the Iguana.* New York: PowerKids Press, 2009.

Enchanted Learning: Iguanas
http://www.enchantedlearning.com/subjects/reptiles/lizard/Iguanaprintout.shtml

San Diego Zoo's Animal Bytes: Iguana
http://www.sandiegozoo.org/animalbytes/t-iguana.html

Stewart, Melissa. *Reptiles.* New York: Children's Press, 2001.

Index

Photo Acknowledgments

The images in this book are used with the permission of: © Joe McDonald/Visuals Unlimited, Inc., pp. 1, 25; © David Kuhn/Dwight Kuhn Photography, p. 2; © Gerald & Buff Corsi/Visuals Unlimited, Inc., pp. 4, 23; © Ted Levin/Animals Animals, p. 5; © Daniel Heuclin/NHPA/ Photoshot, pp. 6, 10; © Joe McDonald, pp. 7, 11; © age fotostock/SuperStock, p. 8; © Wernher Krutein/photovault.com, p. 9; © Dan Suzio/Photo Researchers, Inc., pp. 12, 13, 15; © Stone Nature Photography/Woodfall/Photoshot, pp. 14, 27; © Photos.com/Jupiterimages Corporation, p. 16; © Zigmund Leszczynski/Animals Animals, p. 17; © John Hoffman/Bruce Coleman Inc./Photoshot, p. 18; © John Cancalosi/Alamy, p. 19; © Dan Suzio/Animals Animals, p. 20; © Maslowski/Visuals Unlimited, Inc., p. 21; © blickwinkel/Alamy, p. 22; © Tom McHugh/ Photo Researchers, Inc., p. 24; Dr. Allan Muth, Boyd Deep Canyon Desert Research Center, p. 26; © Laura Westlund/Independent Picture Service, pp. 28, 29; © Steve Strickland/Visuals Unlimited, Inc., p. 31.

Front Cover: © Wernher Krutein/photovault.com (main); © Ron and Patty Thomas/Taxi/Getty Images (background).